Ten of the Best: Stories of Exploration and Adventure

TEN OF THE BEST ADVENTURES IN

Crabtree Publishing Company

www.crabtreebooks.com

Crabtree Publishing Company
www.crabtreebooks.com
1-800-387-7650

Publishing in Canada
616 Welland Ave.
St. Catharines, ON
L2M 5V6

Published in the United States
PMB 59051, 350 Fifth Ave.
59th Floor,
New York, NY

Published in **2016 by CRABTREE PUBLISHING COMPANY.**

Printed in Canada/082015/BF20150630

Photo Credit: Page 22, WPPilot

Project development, design, and concept:
    David West Children's Books

Author and designer: David West

Illustrator: David West

Contributing editor: Steve Parker

Editor: Kathy Middleton

Proofreader: Rebecca Sjonger

**Production coordinator
    and prepress technician**: Ken Wright

Print coordinator: Margaret Amy Salter

Library and Archives Canada Cataloguing in Publication

West, David, 1956-, author
        Ten of the best adventures in space / David West.

(Ten of the best : stories of exploration and adventure)
Includes index.
Issued in print and electronic formats.
ISBN 978-0-7787-1836-9 (bound).--
ISBN 978-0-7787-1842-0 (paperback).--
ISBN 978-1-4271-7804-6 (pdf).--ISBN 978-1-4271-7798-8 (html)

        1. Manned space flight--History--Juvenile literature. 2. Space
flights--Juvenile literature. 3. Astronautics--History--Juvenile
literature. 4. Astronauts--Juvenile literature. I. Title. II. Title:
Adventures in space.

TL793.W46 2015   j629.45009   C2015-903148-6
                                                C2015-903149-4

Library of Congress Cataloging-in-Publication Data

CIP available at the Library of Congress

CONTENTS

First Spaceman

Yuri Gagarin

On April 12, 1961, a young girl runs through a field screaming for her mother. Looking up, her mother sees a strange figure approaching, dressed in orange and wearing a white helmet. The figure assures her that he is a **Soviet** and explains that his name is Yuri Gagarin—and he has just returned from space.

Early in the morning of April 12, **cosmonaut** Yuri Gagarin is strapped into the Vostok 3KA space capsule. The hatch is sealed. The Soviet Union is sending the first human into space for one **orbit** around Earth. At 9:07 a.m. the rockets fire. Gagarin's voice comes over the radio: "Let's go!"

Two minutes into the flight, the used-up rocket boosters fall away. After ten minutes, Vostok has reached outer space. The rocket, no longer needed, separates from the capsule. Gagarin is traveling at 16,777 mph (27,000 kph). He feels the effects of weightlessness and reports how he feels and what he sees out of the small window as he travels around Earth. At 10:25 a.m. the **retro-rockets** fire to slow the craft down for reentry.

As Vostok reenters Earth's atmosphere, **friction** between the spacecraft and the gases surrounding the planet causes the craft to heat up. This is expected, but something is wrong. The spacecraft spins wildly. The equipment module has not detached completely from the Gagarin's module. Still held together by cables, they spin around each other, creating huge **g-forces**. The powerful pressure threatens to cause Gagarin to black out. The capsule gets hotter as its outer layers are burned away. At 10:35 a.m. the cables burn through and the two modules finally separate. Twenty minutes later, there is a loud explosion

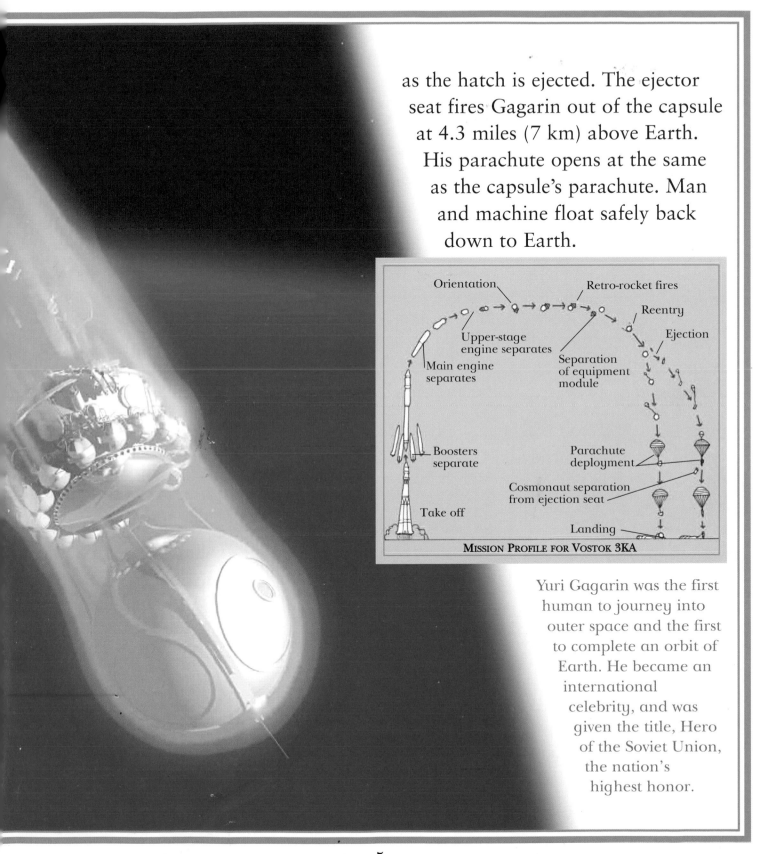

as the hatch is ejected. The ejector seat fires Gagarin out of the capsule at 4.3 miles (7 km) above Earth. His parachute opens at the same as the capsule's parachute. Man and machine float safely back down to Earth.

Orientation

Retro-rocket fires

Reentry

Ejection

Upper-stage engine separates

Main engine separates

Separation of equipment module

Boosters separate

Parachute deployment

Cosmonaut separation from ejection seat

Take off

Landing

MISSION PROFILE FOR VOSTOK 3KA

Yuri Gagarin was the first human to journey into outer space and the first to complete an orbit of Earth. He became an international celebrity, and was given the title, Hero of the Soviet Union, the nation's highest honor.

Escape from Drowning

Virgil "Gus" Grissom

Shortly after Gagarin's space flight, the United States launched its first astronaut, Alan Shepard, into space on May 5, 1961. It was a 15-minute flight that took the capsule up to an **altitude** of 116 miles (187 km). It returned to Earth without completing an orbit.

On July 21, 1961, the second Mercury spacecraft, the *Liberty Bell 7*, was launched into space. It was piloted by astronaut Virgil "Gus" Grissom. The flight lasted 15 minutes and 30 seconds, and reached an altitude of 118 miles (190 km) before splashing down in the Atlantic Ocean.

The flight had been a success until emergency explosive bolts suddenly fired, unexpectedly blowing the capsule's hatch cover into the ocean. Water started flowing into the capsule threatening to sink the craft. Grissom had already unstrapped himself from the safety harness, and he made a hasty exit through the open hatch. For a while he became tangled up in lines, which kept him attached to the sinking capsule. He eventually freed himself and swam clear.

Floating in the sea, Grissom was still not out of danger. He had not closed the air inlet port in his space suit, through which air is let in—and out. He was losing valuable air that could keep him afloat. In the meantime, a rescue helicopter had attached a line to the capsule but was having difficulty lifting it because seawater was pouring into it. Unaware of Grissom's difficulty, none of the helicopters surrounding him dropped him a lifeline.

Grissom had to swim to keep from sinking and was becoming exhausted. Finally, a helicopter dropped him a horse collar, which he just managed to wrestle over his arms and head before being winched to safety. The helicopter took him to the waiting aircraft carrier. The *Liberty Bell* sank to the ocean floor and was not recovered until 1999.

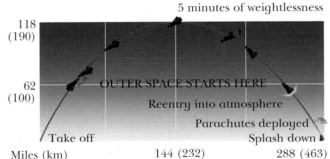

5 minutes of weightlessness

118 (190)

62 (100)

OUTER SPACE STARTS HERE

Reentry into atmosphere

Parachutes deployed

Take off

Splash down

Miles (km)   144 (232)   288 (463)

Spacewalking

Alexey Leonov

In March 1965, the Voskhod 2 space mission blasted off from Baikonur Cosmodrome in Kazakhstan, carrying Soviet cosmonauts Pavel Belyayev and Alexey Leonov. It was to become another major milestone in the history of space travel—and another feather in the cap of the Soviets in the **Space Race**.

The spacecraft was a Vostok-style capsule, upgraded with an air lock—a passageway that keeps air pressure stable for breathing—that could be inflated in orbit. The mission's ambitious goal was to perform the first-ever walk in space. Once in orbit, Belyayev attached an extravehicular activity, or **EVA**, backpack to Leonov's space suit. This would provide 45 minutes of oxygen. Belyayev then extended the inflatable air lock.

Leonov entered the air lock, then Belyayev sealed the spacecraft behind him and depressurized the air lock. Leonov opened the air lock's outer hatch and pushed himself out into space. Secured to the spacecraft by a 17.6-foot (5.4 m) cord, he attached one camera to the spacecraft to record his spacewalk. When he tried to turn on a second camera attached to his chest, he was unable to reach the switch. The air pressure inside his space suit had ballooned it out so that bending the joints became impossible. After 12 minutes and 9 seconds, Leonov retrieved the camera from the spacecraft and returned to the air lock. But his puffed-out space suit prevented him from getting back in, and he got stuck.

Risking **decompression sickness**, Leonov had to reduce the pressure in his suit to an unsafe level. This allowed him to bend his joints and finally reenter the spacecraft.

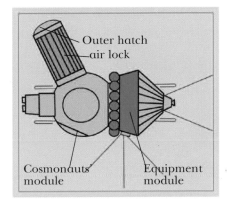

Outer hatch
air lock

Cosmonauts'
module

Equipment
module

The cosmonauts' troubles did not end there. After explosive bolts were fired to discard the air lock, the automatic landing system malfunctioned and they were forced to land it manually. During the reentry, the cosmonauts' module failed to disconnect from the equipment module on time, causing the spacecraft to spin wildly. The spacecraft landed safely—but 240 miles (386 km) from the intended landing zone. The cosmonauts then had to endure a freezing night alone in their capsule, surrounded by wolves and bears, before a rescue party was able to reach them.

Running out of Fuel

Armstrong, Collins, and Aldrin

On July 16, 1969, the giant Saturn V rocket of the American Apollo 11 mission launched three men on a journey to the Moon. The astronauts were Neil Armstrong, Michael Collins, and Edwin "Buzz" Aldrin.

After one and a half orbits of Earth, the engine fired the spacecraft onto its journey toward the Moon. Thirty minutes later, the last Saturn V stage separated. The lunar module—the craft for landing on the Moon—combined with the command/service modules—crafts for returning the astronauts to Earth and for housing power equipment—continued toward the Moon.

On July 19, Apollo 11 reached the Moon and entered lunar orbit. The next day the lunar module, *Eagle*, with Armstrong and Aldrin onboard, separated from the command module. Collins remained in the command module as the *Eagle* made its descent to a plain on the Moon's surface called the Sea of Tranquility.

Noting they were passing landmarks on the surface four seconds sooner than planned, the astronauts realized they would overshoot the landing site. Alarms suddenly went off from the navigation and guidance computer. Armstrong looked out the window again and saw their landing site was strewn with boulders. A low-fuel warning sounded, and Armstrong decided to take control of the *Eagle*. With Aldrin calling out height and speed, Armstrong

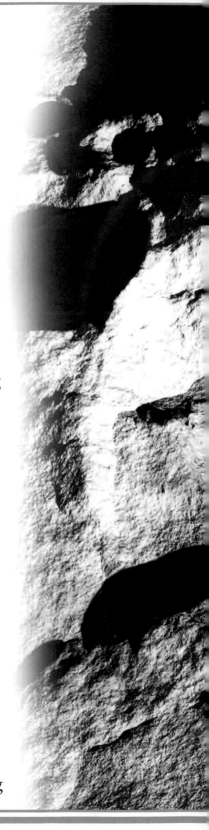

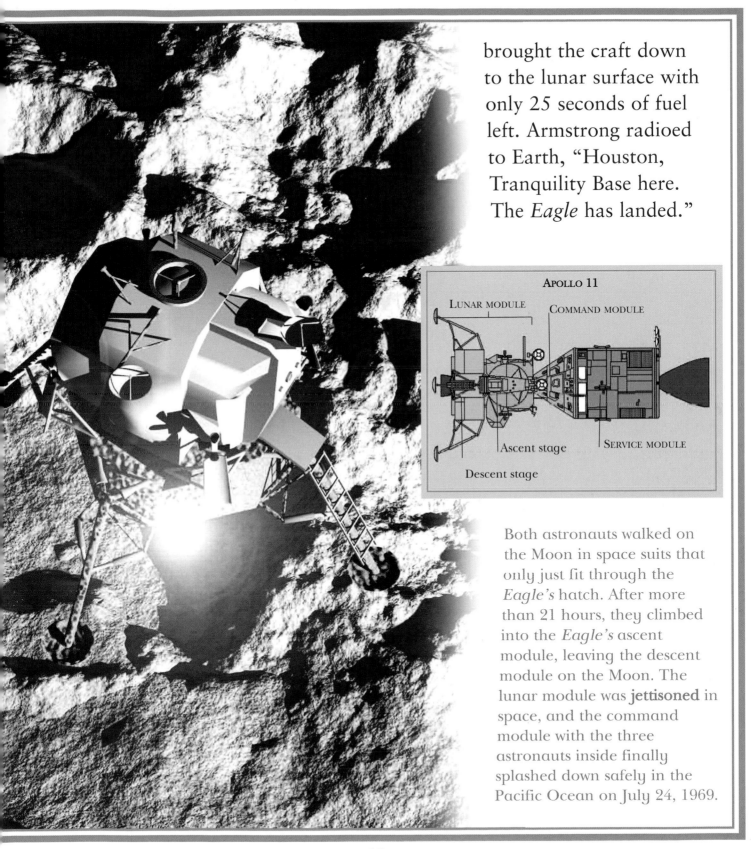

brought the craft down to the lunar surface with only 25 seconds of fuel left. Armstrong radioed to Earth, "Houston, Tranquility Base here. The *Eagle* has landed."

APOLLO 11

LUNAR MODULE

COMMAND MODULE

Ascent stage

SERVICE MODULE

Descent stage

Both astronauts walked on the Moon in space suits that only just fit through the *Eagle's* hatch. After more than 21 hours, they climbed into the *Eagle's* ascent module, leaving the descent module on the Moon. The lunar module was **jettisoned** in space, and the command module with the three astronauts inside finally splashed down safely in the Pacific Ocean on July 24, 1969.

Unlucky 13

James Lovell, John Swigert, and Fred Haise

On April 13, 1970, Apollo 13 (the third Apollo trip to the Moon) was 56 hours into its mission. On board were **NASA** astronauts James Lovell, John Swigert, and Fred Haise. They were 205,000 miles (330,000 km) above Earth when they heard a loud bang, which was followed by changes in electrical power. The crew at first thought that a meteoroid had hit the lunar module, but it soon became clear that part of the service module had exploded.

A short circuit had caused an oxygen tank to explode. The fire and pressure burned up all the fuel cells and oxygen in the service module and blew off the outer panel. This left the command module, *Odyssey*, with limited battery power and water. Landing on the Moon would not happen. The crew would need all of *Odyssey's* power to reenter Earth's atmosphere, so they moved into the lunar module, *Aquarius*. The only way back to Earth was to use the Moon's gravity to slingshot the spacecraft around it so they could coast back home.

Aquarius was designed to support two people for a day and a half—not three people for four days. There was enough oxygen, but electrical power and water had to be managed carefully. The buildup of carbon dioxide was another serious problem. The gas had to be removed for life support, but the extra canisters from *Odyssey* did not fit the filter in *Aquarius*. NASA scientists told the crew how to rig up a filter using tape, tubes, and the wrong-size canisters.

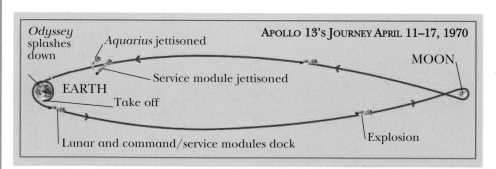

Odyssey splashes down
Aquarius jettisoned
APOLLO 13'S JOURNEY APRIL 11–17, 1970
Service module jettisoned
MOON
EARTH
Take off
Lunar and command/service modules dock
Explosion

As Apollo 13 neared Earth, the service module was jettisoned. The crew moved back into *Odyssey*, then separated from *Aquarius*. *Odyssey* splashed down safely in the South Pacific Ocean on April 17, 1970.

Vasili Lazarev and Oleg Makarov

Balanced on a Cliff's Edge

Soviet cosmonauts Vasili Lazarev and Oleg Makarov blasted off in Soyuz 18-1 on April 5, 1975, for a two-month stay on the Salyut 4 space station.

Their journey toward space began without any problems. But when they reached a height of 90 miles (145 km), things started to go wrong very quickly. The first-stage rocket should have separated from the upper stage, but that did not happen. When the upper stage ignited on time, the thrust from its engine separated the stages, but the force threw the spacecraft off its planned flight path. The onboard computers detected a change beyond the safety limits and automatically started an abort program.

The cosmonauts wondered what was going wrong as a loud siren suddenly sounded and the "Failure" light on an instrument panel glowed red. They experienced weightlessness as the spacecraft slowed. At the edge of space, the descent module containing the two men was released, and it plunged back to Earth. All the two cosmonauts could do was grit their teeth as they were subjected to forces 21 times that of gravity.

The descent module's parachute opened as intended and Soyuz 18-1 drifted down to the snow-covered Altai Mountains. But the cosmonauts were not out of danger yet. As they hit the ground, the capsule landed on a slope and began to slide toward a sheer precipice.

By an amazing stroke of luck, the parachute got caught on some vegetation, which stopped the spacecraft with the two men inside from plunging over the edge of the cliff.

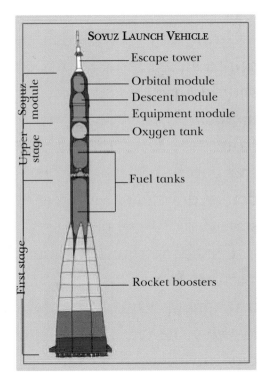

SOYUZ LAUNCH VEHICLE

- Escape tower
- Orbital module
- Descent module
- Equipment module
- Oxygen tank
- Fuel tanks
- Rocket boosters

Soyuz module

Upper stage

First stage

The cosmonauts still had to endure temperatures of 19.4°F (-7°C) until the rescue team arrived by helicopter the next day. Makarov made a full recovery and flew two more missions, but Lazarev had suffered internal injuries and never flew into space again.

Space Shuttle Disaster

(back row) Ellison Onizuka, Christa McAuliffe, Gregory Jarvis, Judith Resnik; *Michael J. Smith, Dick Scobee, Ronald McNair;*

On April 12, 1981, a new type of spacecraft took off from the Kennedy Space Center in Florida. The first space shuttle, called *Columbia*, orbited Earth 37 times, carrying a crew of two—mission commander John Young and pilot Robert Crippen. After 54.5 hours it returned through the atmosphere and glided back to Edwards Air Force Base in California.

The space shuttle was the first reusable space rocket. The shuttle was attached to an external fuel tank and two solid-fuel rocket boosters or SRBs. About two minutes after lift-off, the SRBs would be released, which then parachuted into the ocean to be retrieved and reused. The external fuel tank was the only part that was not reused. It would burn up in the atmosphere after being jettisoned. Six space shuttles were built, with five of them used on 135 missions carrying satellites, space probes, and laboratories into space.

The space shuttle had a clean safety record until January 28, 1986, when NASA's space shuttle orbiter *Challenger* took off on its tenth mission. Seventy-three seconds into the flight, a seal on one of the SRBs failed and a jet of burning fuel caused the external fuel tank to blow up. Engulfed in a fireball, the orbiter veered off, creating such enormous pressure on it that the orbiter rapidly disintegrated as it fell into the ocean. All seven crew members were lost.

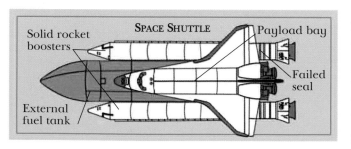

Solid rocket boosters

SPACE SHUTTLE

Payload bay

Failed seal

External fuel tank

A second space shuttle disaster occurred on February 1, 2003. Tiles on the left wing of *Columbia* had been damaged during launch. Hot gases destroyed the wing's inside structure on reentry, breaking the shuttle apart. All crew members were killed. The last space shuttle flew in 2011 before all shuttles were retired.

Shuttle to the Rescue

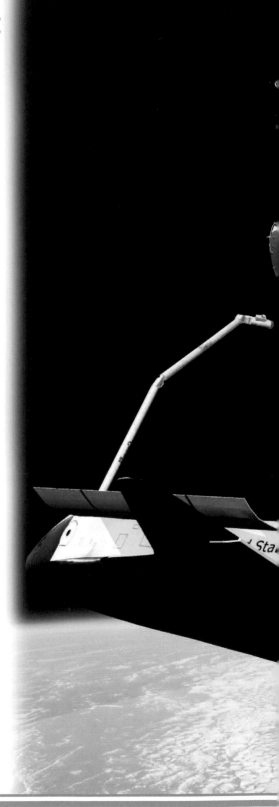

Standing: Covey, Hoffman, Akers; seated: Bowersox, Thornton, Musgrave, Nicollier

In 1990, the space shuttle *Discovery* launched the Hubble Space Telescope into orbit around Earth. Although the mission was a success, it was soon discovered that Hubble had a serious problem. The main mirror had been ground to the wrong shape. Images being sent back to Earth were fuzzy.

Regular servicing was part of the Hubble program's plan. The first shuttle flight to service the telescope was scheduled for 1993, but the astronauts would need to undertake extensive training to be able to correct the optical system. Seven astronauts were trained to use over 100 different tools for a variety of jobs. These included giving the space telescope an optical correction system, as well as replacing the solar panels, four **gyroscopes**, numerous electronic components, and upgrading the onboard computers.

The mission to repair Hubble was one of the most complex in the shuttle's history. Once in orbit the crew of *Endeavour* performed a series of tests that allowed the shuttle to close in on the Hubble Telescope. Commander Dick Covey

maneuvered *Endeavour* to within 30 feet (9.1 m) of Hubble before mission specialist Claude Nicollier used *Endeavour*'s robotic arm to grab the telescope and bring it into the cargo bay.

Two teams of astronauts made five spacewalks to repair the telescope. Some of the walks lasted more than seven hours. In total, the crew spent 35 hours and 28 minutes outside the spacecraft.

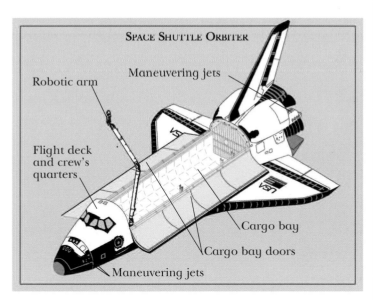

SPACE SHUTTLE ORBITER

Robotic arm

Maneuvering jets

Flight deck and crew's quarters

Cargo bay

Cargo bay doors

Maneuvering jets

On the ninth day of the flight the work was completed. The telescope was released from the shuttle's cargo bay as Commander Dick Covey and Pilot Ken Bowersox fired *Endeavour*'s small maneuvering jets and moved the shuttle away. Eleven days after launch, the shuttle landed back at Kennedy Space Center. A month later, sharp images received from Hubble showed the mission had been a complete success.

Fire in Space

Jerry Linenger

Assembled in orbit from 1986 to 1996, Mir was the first continuously manned, long-term space station. Owned by the Soviet Union, then by Russia after the Soviet Union's breakup, most of the crew members were Russian. But with the Space Race over, Mir, which means "peace" in Russian, was visited by astronauts from North America, Europe, India, and Japan. It was capable of supporting as many as six crew members for up to a month.

On January 12, 1997, American astronaut, Jerry Linenger joined Russian Mir crew members Valeri Korzun and Alexander Kaleri for a five-month stay. On February 12, new crew arrived—Russians Vasily Tsibliev and Aleksandr Lazutkin, and German Reinhold Ewald. With six people onboard Mir was crowded.

On February 24, all six crew members were finishing dinner in the core module, where the living area is. Linenger left to do some work in the Spektr module, where Earth's environment is observed. Suddenly the master alarm went off. As he made his way back to the others, Linenger noticed the first wisps of smoke. He put on a mask. It failed to work, so he grabbed another. Very quickly, the smoke was thick. A three-foot (1 m) flame was shooting out from an oxygen canister, with molten metal flying out of it. Korzun was trying to put out the fire with extinguishers, but they had no effect. The situation had changed from routine to terrifying in an instant. The fire blocked the path to one of the two Soyuz spacecraft, leaving an escape route for only three people.

The oxygen canister eventually burned itself out. The crew found several melted cables, but all Mir's systems continued to operate. Mir was put out of service in 2001 and broke up on reentry.

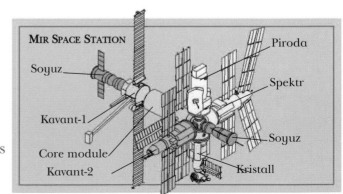

MIR SPACE STATION
Piroda
Soyuz
Spektr
Kavant-1
Soyuz
Core module
Kavant-2
Kristall

Winning the X Prize

Mike Melvill

In May 1996, a space competition, called the Ansari X Prize, was launched offering a $10 million (U.S.) prize. It would be awarded to the first non-government organization to launch a reusable, manned spacecraft into space twice within two weeks. The spacecraft had to be able to carry three people to 62 miles (100 kilometers) above Earth's surface. Twenty-six teams from around the world competed for the prize.

On June 21, 2004, the carrier jet *White Knight* took off with *SpaceShipOne* attached to its underside. American pilot Mike Melvill was at the controls to take the private spaceplane for a test flight. When the jet reached 8.9 miles (14.3 km), *SpaceShipOne* separated from the carrier and immediately ignited its rocket engine. At about 11.4 miles (18.3 km), a high wind suddenly made the spaceplane roll 90 degrees to the left. Melvill corrected the roll but immediately rolled 90 degrees to the right. He leveled out the craft and continued upward toward space, still battling to keep it level. Then the pilot heard a loud bang from the exhaust nozzle. He reported it to ground control, but no problems resulted and he continued to climb.

At 34.1 miles (54.9 km)—and at nearly three times the speed of sound—the rocket engine burned out, as expected. As *SpaceShipOne* continued on a curving course, it reached an altitude of 62.2 miles (100.1 km). Melvill experienced about three and a half minutes of weightlessness—and became the first private astronaut to reach space.

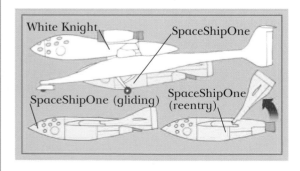

SpaceShipOne's wings could be reshaped in flight. The pilot changed the wing shape as the craft reentered the atmosphere, then changed the shape again to glide and come in for a safe landing. On September 29, 2004, Melvill flew *SpaceShipOne* in the first of its two flights in the X Prize competition. Brian Binnie piloted the second flight on October 4, 2004, to an altitude of 69.6 miles (112 km). The X Prize had been won.

Glossary

altitude A measurement of vertical distance

control thrusters Small nozzles that fire jets of gas to move a spaceship

cosmonaut An astronaut of the Soviet Union or Russia

decompression sickness Bubbles of gas forming in the bloodstream due to change in pressure in the atmosphere

EVA Extra Vehicular Activity, also called a spacewalk

friction Resistance created when one body rubs against another

g-force A type of acceleration that causes stress and strain that feels like weight on people

gyroscope An instrument that aids a person's sense of direction

jettison To cast out of a spacecraft

NASA National Aeronautics and Space Administration; the American space agency

orbit The path of an object around a star, planet, or moon

retro-rockets Rockets that slow a spacecraft

Soviet A citizen of the Soviet Union, a country which existed between 1922 and 1991, when it broke up to become Russia and other countries

Space Race A competition from 1955 to 1972 between the United States and the Soviet Union to be leaders in space exploration

Index